NEW YORK TEST PREP

Practice Test Book

Common Core Math

Grade 4

ISBN 978-1495210471

CONTENTS

INTRODUCTION
For Parents, Teachers, and Tutors

About the Book

This test book contains two complete New York Mathematics Common Core tests. The tests are just like the tests given by the state of New York. Each test contains the same question types and styles, tests the same skills, and has the same length as the state test. If the student can master the math tests in this book, they will be prepared and ready for the real tests.

Taking the Test

The actual New York math test is divided into three books, as described below. This practice test book also divides each test into three books. To mimic the actual test, students should complete one book each day.

Book	Questions	Suggested Time	Maximum Time Allowed
1	25 multiple-choice questions	40 minutes	60 minutes
2	25 multiple-choice questions	40 minutes	60 minutes
3	6 short-response questions 4 extended-response questions	70 minutes	90 minutes

Recording Answers

For books 1 and 2, students can answer the questions by filling in the circle of their answer choice in the test book. Students can also answer the questions by filling in the circles on the optional answer sheet in the back of the book. For book 3, students should write their answers in the test book.

INTRODUCTION
For Parents, Teachers, and Tutors

Question Types

There are three types of questions found on the state test.

- **Multiple-choice** – students select the correct answer from four options.

- **Short-response** – students provide a brief answer and are usually required to show their work.

- **Extended-response** – students complete a more extensive problem. Students may have to show their work, write an explanation, or justify their answer.

Calculators and Tools

Students are not allowed to use a calculator when taking the actual state test. These tests should be completed without the use of a calculator. Students are given a ruler and protractor to use for all sections of the test.

Common Core Math Skills

The math test given by the state of New York covers a specific set of skills and knowledge. These are described in the Common Core Learning Standards (CCLS). These standards were introduced to the New York assessments in 2012-2013, and the state tests are now designed to assess whether students have the skills listed in these standards. Just like the real state tests, the questions in this book cover the skills listed in the CCLS.

The answer key identifies the skill tested by each question, as well as the general topic. Use the topics listed in the answer key to determine areas of strength and weakness. Then target revision and instruction accordingly. Use the skills listed in the answer key to identify the specific skills and knowledge that the student is lacking. Then target revision and instruction accordingly.

Common Core Mathematics

Grade 4

Practice Test 1

Book 1

Instructions

Read each question carefully. For each multiple-choice question, fill in the circle for the correct answer.

You may use a ruler to help you answer questions.

You may use a protractor to help you answer questions.

1   What is the perimeter of the rectangle below?

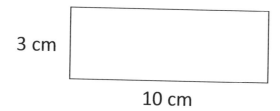

3 cm

10 cm

Ⓐ   13 cm

Ⓑ   30 cm

Ⓒ   26 cm

Ⓓ   60 cm

2   An array for the number 36 is shown below.

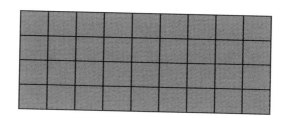

Which number is a factor of 36?

Ⓐ   9

Ⓑ   8

Ⓒ   5

Ⓓ   7

3 The table below shows the cost of food at a diner.

Drinks		Meals	
Small milkshake	$1.80	Plain hamburger	$3.50
Large milkshake	$2.00	Chicken burger	$3.20
Small soda	$1.10	Hotdog	$2.60
Large soda	$1.50	Meatball sub	$3.10
Fruit juice	$1.90	Quiche	$2.10

Lisa bought 2 items and spent exactly $4.00. Which two items could Lisa have bought?

Ⓐ   Meatball sub and a small soda

Ⓑ   Plain hamburger and a large soda

Ⓒ   Chicken burger and a small milkshake

Ⓓ   Quiche and a fruit juice

4   The table below shows the entry cost for a museum.

Adult	$10 per person
Child	$8 per person
Family (2 adults and 2 children)	$30 per family

How much would a family of 2 adults and 2 children save by buying a family ticket instead of individual tickets?

Ⓐ $2

Ⓑ $6

Ⓒ $8

Ⓓ $10

5   Maria is reading a book with 286 pages. She has read 38 pages. To the nearest ten, how many pages does Maria have left to read?

Ⓐ   240

Ⓑ   250

Ⓒ   260

Ⓓ   270

6   A box of beads contains 240 beads. Chang buys 4 boxes of beads. How many beads did Chang buy?

Ⓐ   860

Ⓑ   880   960

Ⓒ   960

Ⓓ   980

7   Liam has 6 pots he grows herbs in. He planted mint in $\frac{1}{4}$ of each pot. What fraction of a pot is the mint in total?

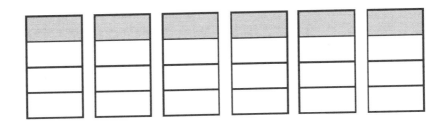

Ⓐ $1\frac{1}{2}$ pots

Ⓑ $1\frac{1}{4}$ pots

Ⓒ $1\frac{1}{6}$ pots

Ⓓ $1\frac{1}{8}$ pots

8   What is the measure of angle *x*?

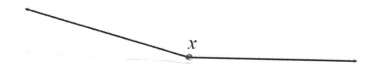

(A)   15°

(B)   25°

(C)   165°

(D)   175°

9   A pet shop sells fish for $3 each. The pet shop sold $96 worth of fish one day. How many fish did the pet shop sell that day?

(A)   32

(B)   36

(C)   48

(D)   288

10 Which number is a factor of 57?

  Ⓐ 11

  Ⓑ 13

  Ⓒ 17

  Ⓓ 19

11 Which number is a multiple of 6?

  Ⓐ 3

  Ⓑ 20

  Ⓒ 36

  Ⓓ 50

12 A motorbike has a weight of 255 kilograms. What is the weight of the motorbike in grams?

  Ⓐ 2,550 grams

  Ⓑ 25,500 grams

  Ⓒ 255,000 grams

  Ⓓ 2,550,000 grams

13 The fraction $\frac{56}{100}$ is plotted on the number line below. What decimal is plotted on the number line?

0.5   0.6

Ⓐ   5.6

Ⓑ   5.06

Ⓒ   0.56

Ⓓ   0.506

14 The table below shows the total number of pieces of bread Aaron used to make peanut butter and jelly sandwiches.

Number of Sandwiches	Number of Pieces of Bread
2	6
4	12
8	24

Which of these describes the relationship in the table?

Ⓐ   Number of sandwiches × 2 = number of pieces of bread

Ⓑ   Number of sandwiches × 3 = number of pieces of bread

Ⓒ   Number of sandwiches × 6 = number of pieces of bread

Ⓓ   Number of sandwiches × 8 = number of pieces of bread

15 The angle that is formed between two lines has a measure of 95°. Which term describes this angle?

Ⓐ   Acute

Ⓑ   Right

Ⓒ   Obtuse

Ⓓ   Straight

16 Jayden wants to find the length of a paperclip. Which unit would Jayden be best to use?

Ⓐ   Yards

Ⓑ   Feet

Ⓒ   Kilometers

Ⓓ   Centimeters

17 There are 1,920 students at Jenna's school. Which of these is another way to write 1,920?

Ⓐ 1,000 + 900 + 20

Ⓑ 1,000 + 900 + 2

Ⓒ 1,000 + 90 + 20

Ⓓ 1,000 + 90 + 2

18 Which of the following describes the rule for this pattern?

1, 3, 6, 8, 11, 13, 16

Ⓐ Add 2, add 3

Ⓑ Add 2, multiply by 2

Ⓒ Multiply by 3, multiply by 2

Ⓓ Multiply by 3, add 3

19 Troy swapped 2 quarters for coins with the same value. Which of these could Troy have swapped his 2 quarters for?

   Ⓐ   25 pennies

   Ⓑ   20 nickels

   Ⓒ   10 nickels

   Ⓓ   10 dimes

20 Which number goes in the box to make the equation below true?

$$54 \div \boxed{} = 9$$

   Ⓐ   5

   Ⓑ   6

   Ⓒ   7

   Ⓓ   8

21 A pumpkin weighs 4 pounds. How many ounces does the pumpkin weigh?

   Ⓐ   32 ounces

   Ⓑ   40 ounces

   Ⓒ   48 ounces

   Ⓓ   64 ounces

22 The table below shows the population of 3 towns.

Town	Population
Franklin	18,725
Torine	24,214
Maxville	16,722

Which number sentence shows the best way to estimate how much greater the population of Torine is than Franklin?

   Ⓐ   24,000 − 16,000 = 8,000

   Ⓑ   24,000 − 17,000 = 7,000

   Ⓒ   24,000 − 18,000 = 6,000

   Ⓓ   24,000 − 19,000 = 5,000

23 A movie made $5,256,374 in its first weekend. What does the 2 in this number represent?

Ⓐ Two thousand

Ⓑ Twenty thousand

Ⓒ Two hundred thousand

Ⓓ Two million

24 Which shape below does **NOT** have a line of symmetry?

Ⓐ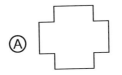

Ⓑ

Ⓒ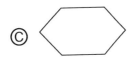

Ⓓ

25   The table shows Davis's phone bill each month.

Month	Amount
April	$9.22
May	$9.09
June	$9.18
July	$9.05

In which month did Davis spend the least on phone calls?

Ⓐ   April

Ⓑ   May

Ⓒ   June

Ⓓ   July

END OF BOOK 1

Common Core Mathematics

Grade 4

Practice Test 1

Book 2

Instructions

Read each question carefully. For each multiple-choice question, fill in the circle for the correct answer.

You may use a ruler to help you answer questions.

You may use a protractor to help you answer questions.

---

26 Emma grouped a set of numbers into two groups, as shown below.

Group 1	Group 2
4	3
6	7
10	17
15	23

Which of these numbers could be added to Group 2?

Ⓐ   25

Ⓑ   26

©   29

Ⓓ   33

27 The sizes of the drill bits in a set are measured in inches. Which size drill bit is greater than $\frac{1}{2}$ inch?

Ⓐ $\frac{3}{8}$ inch

Ⓑ $\frac{7}{16}$ inch

© $\frac{1}{8}$ inch

Ⓓ $\frac{9}{16}$ inch

28 What is the rule to find the value of a term in the sequence below?

Position, n	Value of Term
1	3
2	4
3	5
4	6
5	7

Ⓐ $2n$

Ⓑ $3n$

Ⓒ $n + 2$

Ⓓ $n + 3$

29 A square garden has side lengths of 8 inches. What is the area of the garden?

Ⓐ   32 square inches

Ⓑ   36 square inches

Ⓒ   48 square inches

Ⓓ   64 square inches

30   Look at the line segments shown below.

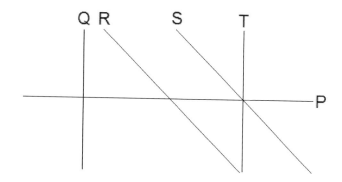

Which two line segments are parallel?

Ⓐ   Line segment P and line segment Q

Ⓑ   Line segment R and line segment S

Ⓒ   Line segment Q and line segment R

Ⓓ   Line segment S and line segment T

31   Which of these is the best estimate of the length of a baseball bat?

Ⓐ   3 inches

Ⓑ   3 feet

Ⓒ   3 millimeters

Ⓓ   3 centimeters

32 There are 40,260 people watching a baseball game. Which of these is another way to write 40,260?

Ⓐ   4 + 2 + 6

Ⓑ   40 + 2 + 60

Ⓒ   40,000 + 200 + 6

Ⓓ   40,000 + 200 + 60

33 The model below is shaded to show $2\frac{4}{10}$.

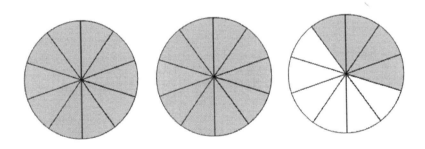

Which decimal does the model represent?

Ⓐ   2.04

Ⓑ   2.4

Ⓒ   0.24

Ⓓ   20.4

34 Which of the following is another way to write the numeral 600,032?

Ⓐ Six hundred thousand and thirty-two

Ⓑ Six million and thirty-two

Ⓒ Six hundred and thirty-two

Ⓓ Six thousand and thirty-two

35 The drawing below shows a kite.

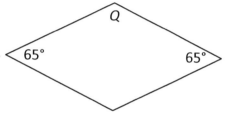

Not drawn to scale

What is the measure of angle *Q*?

Ⓐ 57.5°

Ⓑ 65°

Ⓒ 115°

Ⓓ 230°

36 Which number is a composite number?

Ⓐ 67

Ⓑ 73

Ⓒ 89

Ⓓ 91

37 What is 83,460 rounded to the nearest hundred?

Ⓐ 83,000

Ⓑ 84,000

Ⓒ 83,400

Ⓓ 83,500

38 Which pair of numbers completes the equation below?

Ⓐ 60 and 6,000

Ⓑ 60 and 60,000

Ⓒ 6 and 60

Ⓓ 6 and 6000

39 What is the measure of the angle shown below?

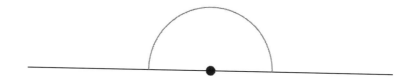

Ⓐ 45°

Ⓑ 90°

Ⓒ 100°

Ⓓ 180°

40 Kai found the coins shown below in the sofa. What is the value of the coins that Kai found?

Ⓐ $1.26

Ⓑ $1.36

Ⓒ $1.45

Ⓓ $2.36

41   Which figure below does NOT have any parallel sides?

Ⓐ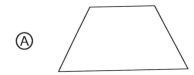

Ⓑ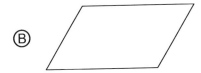

Ⓒ

Ⓓ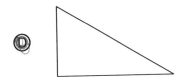

42   What is another way to write the fraction $\frac{9}{4}$?

Ⓐ $1\frac{1}{4}$

Ⓑ $1\frac{3}{4}$

Ⓒ $2\frac{1}{4}$

Ⓓ $2\frac{3}{4}$

43 Jackie made this table to show how much she received in tips on the four days that she worked. On which day did Jackie earn closest to $32?

Day	Amount
Monday	$32.55
Tuesday	$31.98
Thursday	$30.75
Friday	$32.09

Ⓐ   Monday

Ⓑ   Tuesday

Ⓒ   Thursday

Ⓓ   Friday

44 Bruce is counting his quarters. He puts them in 35 piles of 5. How could you work out the total value of the quarters?

Ⓐ   Divide 35 by 5, and multiply the result by $0.25

Ⓑ   Multiply 35 by 5, and multiply the result by $0.25

Ⓒ   Divide 35 by 5, and divide the result by $0.25

Ⓓ   Multiply 35 by 5, and divide the result by $0.25

45 A bakery makes muffins in batches of 12. The bakery made 18 batches of muffins. Which is the best estimate of the number of muffins made?

    Ⓐ   100

    Ⓑ   400

    Ⓒ   250

    Ⓓ   200

46 Katie saw the sign below at a fruit stand.

If Katie spent $6 on oranges, how many oranges would she get?

    Ⓐ   10

    Ⓑ   12

    Ⓒ   20

    Ⓓ   24

47   The normal price of a CD player is $298. During a sale, the CD player was $45 less than the normal price. What was the sale price of the CD player?

Ⓐ $343

Ⓑ $333

Ⓒ $263

Ⓓ $253

48   Bagels are sold in packets of 4 or packets of 6. Kieran needs to buy exactly 32 bagels. Which set of packets could Kieran buy?

Ⓐ   2 packets of 4 bagels and 4 packets of 6 bagels

Ⓑ   3 packets of 4 bagels and 3 packets of 6 bagels

Ⓒ   4 packets of 4 bagels and 2 packets of 6 bagels

Ⓓ   5 packets of 4 bagels and 1 packet of 6 bagels

49   What is the product of 8 and 9?

    Ⓐ   56

    Ⓑ   64

    Ⓒ   72

    Ⓓ   81

50   A bakery ordered 60 cartons of eggs. There were 12 eggs in each carton. Which number sentence could be used to find e, the total number of eggs the bakery ordered?

    Ⓐ $60 \times 12 = e$

    Ⓑ $60 + 12 = e$

    Ⓒ $60 - 12 = e$

    Ⓓ $60 \div 12 = e$

END OF BOOK 2

Common Core Mathematics

Grade 4

Practice Test 1

Book 3

Instructions

Read each question carefully. Write your answer in the space provided. Be sure to show your work when asked. You may receive partial credit if you have shown your work.

You may use a ruler to help you answer questions.

You may use a protractor to help you answer questions.

51 Jenna buys 8 packets of letter paper. Each packet contains 12 sheets of paper. She uses 16 sheets of letter paper a week. How many weeks will it take her to use all the letter paper?

Show your work.

$$
\begin{array}{r}
96 \\
-\ 16 \\
\hline
80
\end{array}
$$

Answer _____ 86 _____ weeks

52 Kenneth got on a train at 9:30 in the morning. He got off the train at 1:20 in the afternoon. How long was Kenneth on the train for?

Show your work.

Answer _____8_____ hours _____10_____ minutes

53 A fish tank can hold 20 liters of water. How many milliliters of water can the fish tank hold?

Show your work.

Answer __20.0Q6__ ml

54 What is the measure of the angle shown below?

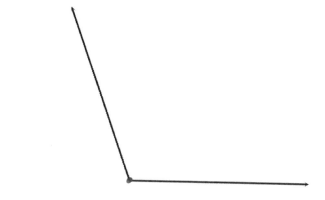

Answer ___110°___

55 The table below shows the number of male and female students at Hill Street School.

Gender	Number
Male	2,629
Female	2,518

Part A

How many students go to the school in all?

Show your work.

2 6 2 9
2 5 1 8
5 1 4 7

Answer 5147

Part B

How many more male students are there than female students?

Show your work.

Answer 111

56   A right triangle is shown below.

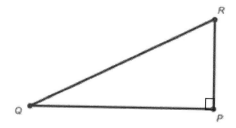

If angle *Q* measures 35°, what is the measure of angle *R*?

Show your work.

Answer _____35_____ °

57   Look at the number line below.

Part A

Plot the decimal 1.75 on the number line.

Part B

What fraction is equivalent to 1.75?

$$1\frac{3}{4}$$

Answer _____

Explain how you found your answer.

The students describe using the number line to determine the fraction

58   Look at the model below.

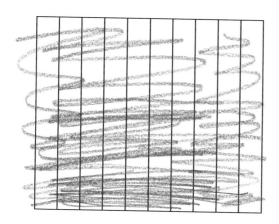 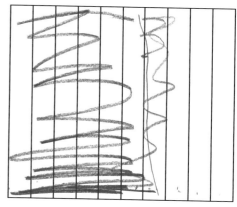

Part A

Shade the model to show $1\frac{7}{10}$.

Part B

Write the mixed number $1\frac{7}{10}$ as an improper fraction.

Answer _____17_____

On the lines below, explain how you found your answer.

I   10 × 1 = 10   then

10 + 7 = 17

59 Look at the number pattern below.

$$5, 11, 17, 23, 29, 35, \underline{41}$$

Part A
If the pattern continues, which number will come next?

Answer __41 7__

Part B
Explain how you found your answer.

I did   add 6

_____

_____

_____

60   Salma drew these shapes.

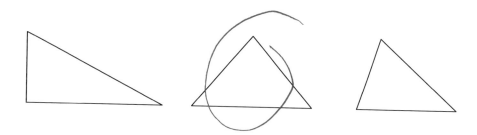

Part A

Circle the shape that has a line of symmetry.

Part B

On the lines below, describe how you can tell that the shape has a line of symmetry.

The   issocles   triangle

a   stringht   line   down

to   pove   it   symmetry

END OF BOOK 3

Common Core Mathematics

Grade 4

Practice Test 2

Book 1

Instructions

Read each question carefully. For each multiple-choice question, fill in the circle for the correct answer.

You may use a ruler to help you answer questions.

You may use a protractor to help you answer questions.

1   Josephine boarded a train at 10:10 a.m. She got off the train at 12:55 p.m. How many minutes was she on the train for?

    Ⓐ   105 minutes

    Ⓑ   165 minutes

    Ⓒ   205 minutes

    Ⓓ   245 minutes

2   Ari is putting photos in an album. He can fit 6 photos on each page. He has 44 photos to place in the album. If he puts 6 photos on each page and the remainder on the last page, how many photos will be on the last page?

    Ⓐ   1

    Ⓑ   2

    Ⓒ   3

    Ⓓ   4

3   Which is a prime factor of the composite number 24?

   Ⓐ   8

   Ⓑ   7

   Ⓒ   6

   Ⓓ   3

4   Mia is setting up tables for a party. Each table can seat 6 people. Mia needs to seat 36 people. Mia wants to find how many tables she will need. Which equation could be solved to find the number of tables, t, that Mia needs?

   Ⓐ $6 \times t = 36$

   Ⓑ $6 \div t = 36$

   Ⓒ $t + 6 = 36$

   Ⓓ $t - 6 = 36$

5   Vienna bought a packet of 12 gift cards. She used 2 gift cards and her sister used 3 gift cards. What fraction of the gift cards did the two sisters use?

Ⓐ $\dfrac{1}{2}$

Ⓑ $\dfrac{2}{3}$

Ⓒ $\dfrac{5}{12}$

Ⓓ $\dfrac{1}{6}$

6   Zoe has 90 small lollipops, 30 large lollipops, and 55 candies.

What is a common factor Zoe could use to divide the treats into equal groups?

Ⓐ   3

Ⓑ   5

Ⓒ   10

Ⓓ   15

7   A school cafeteria offered four Italian meal choices. The table below shows the number of meals served of each type.

Meal	Number Served
Pasta	151
Pizza	167
Salad	213
Risotto	117

Which is the best estimate of the total number of meals served?

Ⓐ   630

Ⓑ   650

Ⓒ   660

Ⓓ   670

8   Jay made 8 trays of 6 muffins each. He gave 12 muffins away. Which expression can be used to find how many muffins he had left?

Ⓐ $(8 \times 6) - 12$

Ⓑ $(8 \times 6) + 12$

Ⓒ $8 + 6 - 12$

Ⓓ $8 + 6 + 12$

9   Stevie had $1.45. She bought a drink for $1.20. Stevie was given one coin as change. Which coin should Stevie have been given?

Ⓐ   A dime

Ⓑ   A penny

Ⓒ   A quarter

Ⓓ   A nickel

10   Which of these is the best estimate of the mass of a watermelon?

Ⓐ   5 ounces

Ⓑ   5 grams

Ⓒ   5 pounds

Ⓓ   5 milligrams

11   The factor tree for the number 60 is shown below.

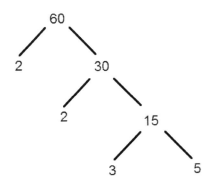

According to the factor tree, which statement is true?

Ⓐ   The number 30 is prime.

Ⓑ   The only prime factor of 60 is 2.

Ⓒ   The numbers 15 and 30 are prime factors of 60.

Ⓓ   The numbers 2, 3, and 5 are prime factors of 60.

12 Each number that was put into the number machine below changed according to a rule.

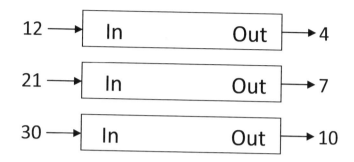

Which equation describes the rule for the number machine?

Ⓐ   Number in × 3 = number out

Ⓑ   Number in + 20 = number out

Ⓒ   Number in ÷ 3 = number out

Ⓓ   Number in − 8 = number out

13 Malcolm surveyed some people to find out how many pets they owned. The line plot shows the results of the survey.

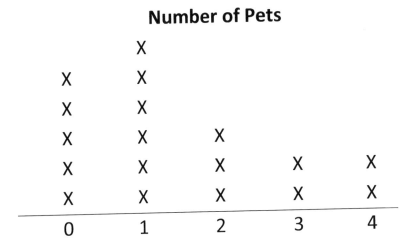

How many people owned 2 or more pets?

Ⓐ 3

Ⓑ 4

Ⓒ 7

Ⓓ 9

14   The shaded model below represents a fraction.

Which model below represents an equivalent fraction?

Ⓐ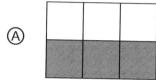

Ⓑ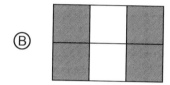

Ⓒ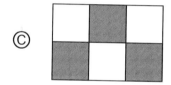

Ⓓ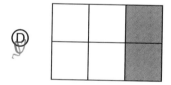

15   Which digit is in the thousands place in the number 6,124,853?

Ⓐ   6

Ⓑ   1

Ⓒ   2

Ⓓ   4

16   Which decimal does the shaded model below represent?

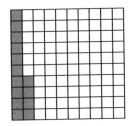

   &Ⓐ   1.4

   Ⓑ   0.014

   Ⓒ   0.14

   Ⓓ   14.0

17   The diagram shows two sets of black and white stickers.

Which of the following compares the portion of black stickers in each set?

   Ⓐ $\dfrac{8}{9} > \dfrac{2}{3}$

   Ⓑ $\dfrac{8}{9} < \dfrac{2}{9}$

   Ⓒ $\dfrac{2}{3} < \dfrac{1}{3}$

   Ⓓ $\dfrac{1}{9} > \dfrac{6}{9}$

18 The grade 4 students at Diane's school are collecting cans for a food drive. The table below shows how many cans each class collected.

Class	Number of Cans
Miss Adams	36
Mr. Walsh	28
Mrs. Naroda	47

Which is the best way to estimate the number of cans collected in all?

Ⓐ 30 + 20 + 40 = ?

Ⓑ 30 + 30 + 40 = ?

Ⓒ 40 + 30 + 50 = ?

Ⓓ 40 + 30 + 40 = ?

19 Which measurement is equal to 12 pints?

Ⓐ 3 quarts

Ⓑ 6 quarts

Ⓒ 24 quarts

Ⓓ 48 quarts

20 What is the measure of the smallest angle of the triangle below?

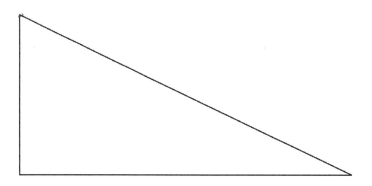

Ⓐ 15°

Ⓑ 25°

Ⓒ 55°

Ⓓ 65°

21 If *n* is a number in the pattern, which rule can be used to find the next number in the pattern?

4, 6, 8, 10, 12, 14, 16, ...

Ⓐ *n* + 2

Ⓑ *n* − 2

Ⓒ *n* + 4

Ⓓ *n* − 4

22   What part of the model is shaded?

   Ⓐ   0.01

   Ⓑ   0.1

   Ⓒ   1

   Ⓓ   10

23   Which of these shapes has exactly one pair of perpendicular sides?

Ⓐ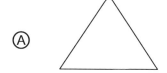

Ⓑ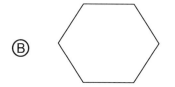

Ⓒ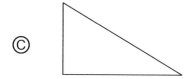

Ⓓ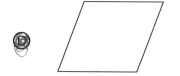

24 Which diagram shows a line of symmetry?

Ⓐ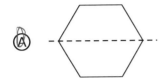

Ⓑ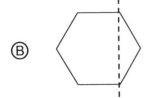

Ⓒ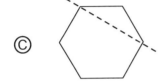

Ⓓ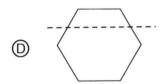

25 Thomas scored 5 times as many points in a basketball game as Jarrod. If Jarrod's number of points is represented as x, which of these shows Thomas's number of points?

Ⓐ $5 + x$

Ⓑ $5 - x$

Ⓒ $\dfrac{5}{x}$

Ⓓ $5x$

END OF BOOK 1

Common Core Mathematics

Grade 4

Practice Test 2

Book 2

Instructions

Read each question carefully. For each multiple-choice question, fill in the circle for the correct answer.

You may use a ruler to help you answer questions.

You may use a protractor to help you answer questions.

---

26 Which of the following is a right triangle?

Ⓐ

Ⓑ

Ⓒ

Ⓓ

27 Madison used $1\frac{3}{4}$ cups of milk to make a milkshake. Which of the following is another way to write $1\frac{3}{4}$?

Ⓐ $\frac{1}{4} + \frac{3}{4}$

Ⓑ $\frac{4}{4} + \frac{3}{4}$

Ⓒ $\frac{1 \times 3}{4}$

Ⓓ $\frac{4 \times 3}{4}$

28   Andy was buying a used car. He had four cars in his price range to choose from. The four cars had the odometer readings listed below.

Car	Chrysler	Ford	Honda	Saturn
Reading (miles)	22,482	21,987	23,689	22,501

If Andy decided to buy the car with the second highest odometer reading, which car would be buy?

Ⓐ   Chrysler

Ⓑ   Ford

Ⓒ   Honda

Ⓓ   Saturn

29   Which number goes in the box to make the equation below true?

$$44 \div \boxed{} = 11$$

Ⓐ   4

Ⓑ   10

Ⓒ   11

Ⓓ   33

30 Which of the following has a mass of about 1 gram?

Ⓐ A dictionary

Ⓑ A pen

Ⓒ A car

Ⓓ A paper clip

31 Which model is shaded to show a fraction equivalent to $\frac{6}{10}$?

Ⓐ

Ⓑ

Ⓒ

Ⓓ

32 Jade made a pattern using marbles. The first four steps of the pattern are shown below.

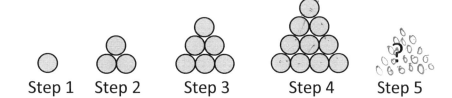

Step 1   Step 2   Step 3   Step 4   Step 5

If Jade continues the pattern, how many marbles will she need for Step 5?

Ⓐ   13

Ⓑ   14

Ⓒ   15

Ⓓ   16

33 A bookstore sold 40,905 books in May. Which of these is another way to write 40,905?

Ⓐ   Four thousand nine hundred and five

Ⓑ   Forty thousand ninety five

Ⓒ   Four thousand ninety five

Ⓓ   Forty thousand nine hundred and five

34 The thermometers below show the air temperature at 10 a.m. and 2 p.m. one day.

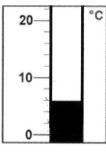

10 a.m.   2 p.m.

How much did the temperature rise by from 10 a.m. to 2 p.m.?

Ⓐ   5°C

Ⓑ   6°C

Ⓒ   10°C

Ⓓ   16°C

35   Which pair of numbers best completes this table?

Number	Number × 10
850	8,500
3,501	35,010
19	190

Ⓐ

28	208

Ⓑ

365	36,500

Ⓒ

1,987	19,870

Ⓓ

6	600

36   The model below shows $2\frac{8}{100}$ shaded.

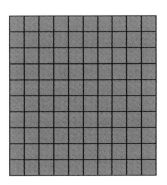 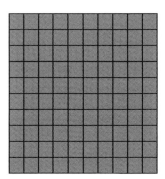 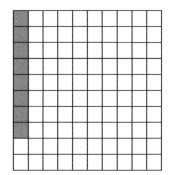

What decimal represents the shaded part of the model?

Ⓐ   2.8

Ⓑ   2.08

Ⓒ   200.8

Ⓓ   200.08

37   Joy started a hike at 1:50. It took Joy 2 hours and 25 minutes to finish the hike. What time did Joy finish the hike?

Ⓐ   3:35

Ⓑ   3:50

Ⓒ   4:05

Ⓓ   4:15

38 Ronald competed in a swimming race. All the students finished the race in between 42.5 seconds and 47.6 seconds. Which of the following could have been Ronald's time?

Ⓐ   41.9 seconds

Ⓑ   40.5 seconds

Ⓒ   46.8 seconds

Ⓓ   48.1 seconds

39 Which procedure can be used to find the next number in the sequence?

120, 60, 30, 15, …

Ⓐ   Subtract 15 from the previous number

Ⓑ   Add 15 to the previous number

Ⓒ   Multiply the previous number by 2

Ⓓ   Divide the previous number by 2

40   Which of these is the best estimate of the mass of an apple?

    Ⓐ   100 milligrams

    Ⓑ   100 grams

    Ⓒ   100 kilograms

    Ⓓ   100 tons

41   Kevin is 1.45 meters tall. Brad is 20 centimeters taller than Kevin. What is Brad's height?

    Ⓐ   1.452 meters

    Ⓑ   1.47 meters

    Ⓒ   1.65 meters

    Ⓓ   21.45 meters

42 Camilla bought 4 bags of apples. Each bag weighed $\frac{3}{8}$ pounds. What was the total weight of the apples?

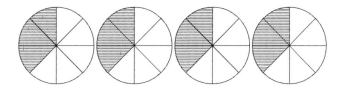

Ⓐ   3 pounds

Ⓑ $1\frac{1}{2}$ pounds

Ⓒ $1\frac{1}{8}$ pounds

Ⓓ $\frac{7}{8}$ pounds

43 Each number in Set P is related in the same way to the number beside it in Set Q.

Set P	Set Q
2	8
6	12
8	14
10	16

When given a number in Set P, what is one way to find its related number in Set Q?

Ⓐ Multiply by 4

Ⓑ Multiply by 2

Ⓒ Add 6

Ⓓ Add 8

44 In which of these does the number 8 make the equation true?

Ⓐ $48 \div \square = 6$

Ⓑ $\square \div 6 = 48$

Ⓒ $48 \times 6 = \square$

Ⓓ $\square \times 48 = 6$

45 There are 30,804 people living in Montville. Which of these is another way to write 30,804?

Ⓐ   30,000 + 800 + 4

Ⓑ   30 + 80 + 4

Ⓒ   3,000 + 800 + 40

Ⓓ   300 + 80 + 4

46 What does the circled area of the diagram show?

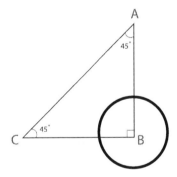

Ⓐ   A ray

Ⓑ   An angle

Ⓒ   A line segment

   A point

47 The line plot below shows how many goals each member of a soccer team scored in the season.

Soccer Goals

```
    X       X
    X       X       X
    X       X       X       X
    X       X       X       X       X
  ─────────────────────────────────────
    0       1       2       3       4
```

Which statement is true?

Ⓐ   Each player scored at least 1 goal.

Ⓑ   Only one player scored more than 3 goals.

Ⓒ   The same number of players scored 2 goals as scored 3 goals.

Ⓓ   More players scored 1 goal than scored no goals.

48 The population of Greenville is 609,023. What does the 9 in this number represent?

Ⓐ   Nine thousand

Ⓑ   Ninety thousand

Ⓒ   Nine hundred thousand

Ⓓ   Ninety

49 Which number is less than 35.052?

Ⓐ 35.009

Ⓑ 35.061

Ⓒ 35.101

Ⓓ 35.077

50 Which fraction and decimal is plotted on the number line below?

Ⓐ $3\frac{4}{5}$ and 3.4

Ⓑ $3\frac{4}{5}$ and 3.8

Ⓒ $3\frac{4}{10}$ and 3.4

Ⓓ $3\frac{4}{10}$ and 3.8

END OF BOOK 2

Common Core Mathematics

Grade 4

Practice Test 2

Book 3

Instructions

Read each question carefully. Write your answer in the space provided. Be sure to show your work when asked. You may receive partial credit if you have shown your work.

You may use a ruler to help you answer questions.

You may use a protractor to help you answer questions.

---

51 What are all the common factors of 10, 20, and 40?

Show your work.

Answer _____

52 Mrs. Smyth has 82 colored pencils. She wants to divide them evenly between 8 people. How many whole pencils will each person receive?

Show your work.

$$8\overline{)82} \quad {}^{1}6\,R2$$

8

0 2

Answer _____10R2_____ pencils

53 The table below shows the number of students in each grade at the David Hall School.

Grade	Number of Students
3	254
4	235
5	229

How many students are there in all?

Show your work.

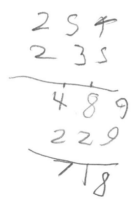

Answer ____758____

54   Karen made this table to show her monthly phone bills.

Month	Amount
April	$5.42
May	$5.39
June	$5.51
July	$5.27

Place the months in order from the lowest bill to the highest bill. Write the months on the lines below.

Lowest   _July_

May

April

Highest   _June_

55   What is the area of the square shown below?

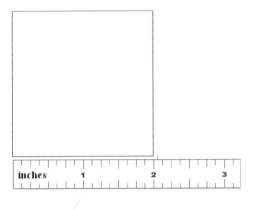

Show your work.

$2 \times 4 = 8 in$

Answer ___8___ inches

56 Jeremy had the coins shown below.

He swapped all the coins for nickels of the same total value. How many nickels should he have received?

Show your work.

Answer _____15_____ nickels

57 Jed has 12 dimes, 18 nickels, and 24 pennies. He wants to divide them into as many piles as possible, but he wants the same number of dimes, nickels, and pennies in each pile.

Part A

What is the greatest number of equal piles Jed can divide the coins into?

Show your work.

Answer _____

Part B

If Jed divides the coins into those equal piles, how many pennies will be in each pile?

Show your work.

Answer _____

58 In the space below, sketch and label a right angle, an acute angle, and an obtuse angle.

Right Angle

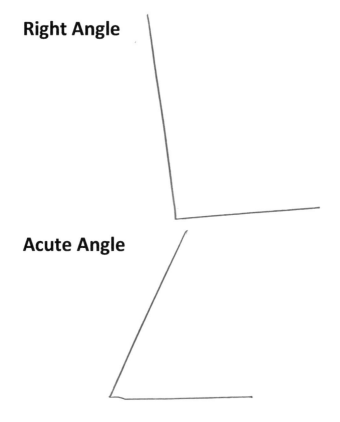

Acute Angle

Obtuse Angle

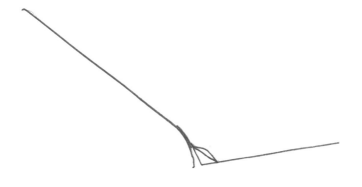

59 Emma grouped the numbers from 10 to 20 into prime and composite numbers.

Prime	Composite
11	10
13	12
17	14
19	15
2 3	16
2 6	18
2 9	20

Which numbers from 21 to 30 should Emma add to the list of prime numbers? List the numbers below.

Answer _____

Explain how the prime numbers are different from composite numbers.

_____

_____

_____

_____

60 A rectangular park has a length of 80 feet and a width of 40 feet.

Part A

What is the perimeter of the park in feet?

Show your work.

3 feet 1 yard

Answer ____240____ feet

$$\frac{240}{3}$$

Part B

What is the perimeter of the park in yards?

3) 240

Show your work.

$$\frac{1 \text{ yards}}{3 \text{ feet}}$$

Answer ____80____ yards

END OF BOOK 3

ANSWER KEY AND SKILLS LIST

Common Core Math Skills

The math test given by the state of New York covers a specific set of skills and knowledge. These are described in the Common Core Learning Standards (CCLS). These standards were introduced to the New York assessments in 2012-2013, and the state tests are now designed to assess whether students have the skills listed in these standards. Just like the real state tests, the questions in this book cover the skills listed in the CCLS.

Assessing Skills and Knowledge

The skills listed in the Common Core Learning Standards are divided into five topics, or clusters. These are:

- Operations and Algebraic Thinking
- Number and Operations in Base Ten
- Number and Operations – Fractions
- Measurement and Data
- Geometry

The answer key identifies the topic for each question. Use the topics listed to identify general areas of strength and weakness. Then target revision and instruction accordingly.

The answer key also identifies the specific math skill that each question is testing. Use the skills listed to identify skills that the student is lacking. Then target revision and instruction accordingly.

Common Core Mathematics, Practice Test 1, Book 1

Question	Answer	Topic	Common Core Skill
1	C	Measurement & Data	Apply the area and perimeter formulas for rectangles in real world and mathematical problems.
2	A	Operations/Algebraic Thinking	Recognize that a whole number is a multiple of each of its factors.
3	D	Measurement & Data	Use the four operations to solve word problems involving money.
4	B	Operations/Algebraic Thinking	Solve multistep word problems posed with whole numbers and having whole-number answers using the four operations.
5	B	Operations/Algebraic Thinking	Assess the reasonableness of answers using mental computation and estimation strategies including rounding.
6	C	Number & Operations in Base Ten	Multiply a whole number of up to four digits by a one-digit whole number using strategies based on place value and the properties of operations.
7	A	Number & Operations-Fractions	Apply and extend previous understandings of multiplication to multiply a fraction by a whole number.
8	C	Measurement & Data	Measure angles in whole-number degrees using a protractor.
9	A	Number & Operations in Base Ten	Find whole-number quotients and remainders with up to four-digit dividends and one-digit divisors.
10	D	Operations/Algebraic Thinking	Find all factor pairs for a whole number in the range 1–100.
11	C	Operations/Algebraic Thinking	Determine whether a given whole number in the range 1–100 is a multiple of a given one-digit number.
12	C	Measurement & Data	Within a single system of measurement, express measurements in a larger unit in terms of a smaller unit.
13	C	Number & Operations-Fractions	Use decimal notation for fractions with denominators 10 or 100.
14	B	Operations/Algebraic Thinking	Generate and analyze patterns.
15	C	Geometry	Draw and identify right, acute, and obtuse angles.
16	D	Measurement & Data	Know relative sizes of measurement units within one system of units.
17	A	Number & Operations in Base Ten	Read and write multi-digit whole numbers using base-ten numerals, number names, and expanded form.
18	A	Operations/Algebraic Thinking	Generate and analyze patterns.
19	C	Measurement & Data	Use the four operations to solve word problems involving money.
20	B	Number & Operations in Base Ten	Find whole-number quotients using strategies based on place value, the properties of operations, and/or the relationship between multiplication and division.

21	D	Measurement & Data	Within a single system of measurement, express measurements in a larger unit in terms of a smaller unit.
22	D	Operations/Algebraic Thinking	Assess the reasonableness of answers using mental computation and estimation strategies including rounding.
23	C	Number & Operations in Base Ten	Recognize that in a multi-digit whole number, a digit in one place represents ten times what it represents in the place to its right.
24	B	Geometry	Identify line-symmetric figures and draw lines of symmetry.
25	D	Number & Operations-Fractions	Compare two decimals to hundredths by reasoning about their size.

Common Core Mathematics, Practice Test 1, Book 2

Question	Answer	Topic	Common Core Skill
26	C	Operations/Algebraic Thinking	Determine whether a given whole number in the range 1–100 is prime or composite.
27	D	Number & Operations-Fractions	Compare two fractions with different numerators and different denominators.
28	C	Operations/Algebraic Thinking	Generate and analyze patterns.
29	D	Measurement & Data	Apply the area and perimeter formulas for rectangles in real world and mathematical problems.
30	B	Geometry	Identify perpendicular and parallel lines in two-dimensional figures.
31	B	Measurement & Data	Know relative sizes of measurement units within one system of units.
32	D	Number & Operations in Base Ten	Read and write multi-digit whole numbers using base-ten numerals, number names, and expanded form.
33	B	Number & Operations-Fractions	Use decimal notation for fractions with denominators 10 or 100.
34	A	Number & Operations in Base Ten	Read and write multi-digit whole numbers using base-ten numerals, number names, and expanded form.
35	C	Measurement & Data	Solve addition and subtraction problems to find unknown angles on a diagram in real world and mathematical problems.
36	D	Operations/Algebraic Thinking	Determine whether a given whole number in the range 1–100 is prime or composite.
37	D	Number & Operations in Base Ten	Use place value understanding to round multi-digit whole numbers to any place.
38	A	Number & Operations in Base Ten	Recognize that in a multi-digit whole number, a digit in one place represents ten times what it represents in the place to its right.
39	D	Measurement & Data	Measure angles in whole-number degrees using a protractor.
40	B	Measurement & Data	Use the four operations to solve word problems involving money.
41	D	Geometry	Identify perpendicular and parallel lines in two-dimensional figures.
42	C	Number & Operations-Fractions	Recognize and generate equivalent fractions.
43	B	Number & Operations-Fractions	Compare two decimals to hundredths by reasoning about their size.
44	B	Number & Operations-Fractions	Solve word problems involving multiplication of a fraction by a whole number.
45	D	Operations/Algebraic Thinking	Assess the reasonableness of answers using mental computation and estimation strategies including rounding.
46	D	Operations/Algebraic Thinking	Solve multistep word problems posed with whole numbers and having whole-number answers using the four operations.
47	D	Number & Operations in Base Ten	Fluently add and subtract multi-digit whole numbers using the standard algorithm.

48	A	Operations/Algebraic Thinking	Solve multistep word problems posed with whole numbers and having whole-number answers using the four operations.
49	C	Number & Operations in Base Ten	Multiply a whole number of up to four digits by a one-digit whole number.
50	A	Operations/Algebraic Thinking	Represent problems using equations with a letter standing for the unknown quantity.

Common Core Mathematics, Practice Test 1, Book 3

Question	Points	Topic	Common Core Skill
51	2	Operations/Algebraic Thinking	Solve multistep word problems posed with whole numbers and having whole-number answers using the four operations.
52	2	Measurement & Data	Use the four operations to solve word problems involving time.
53	2	Measurement & Data	Within a single system of measurement, express measurements in a larger unit in terms of a smaller unit.
54	2	Measurement & Data	Measure angles in whole-number degrees using a protractor.
55	2	Number & Operations in Base Ten	Fluently add and subtract multi-digit whole numbers using the standard algorithm.
56	2	Measurement & Data	Solve addition and subtraction problems to find unknown angles on a diagram in real world and mathematical problems.
57	3	Number & Operations-Fractions	Understand decimal notation for fractions, and compare decimal fractions.
58	3	Number & Operations-Fractions	Build fractions from unit fractions by applying and extending previous understandings of operations on whole numbers.
59	3	Operations/Algebraic Thinking	Generate and analyze patterns.
60	3	Geometry	Recognize a line of symmetry for a two-dimensional figure as a line across the figure such that the figure can be folded along the line into matching parts.

Q51.
Answer
6 weeks

Work
The work should show the calculation of 8 × 12 = 96 and 96 ÷ 16 = 6.

Scoring Information
Give a total score of 0, 1, or 2.
Give a score of 1 for the correct answer.
Give a score of 0 or 1 for the working.

Q52.
Answer
3 hours 50 minutes

Work
The student may find the time from 9:30 to midday and then add the time from midday to 1:20, find the hours from 9:30 to 12:30 and then add the minutes from 12:30 to 1:20, find the hours from 9:30 to 1:30 and then subtract 10 minutes, or find the minutes from 9:30 to 1:20 and then convert the time to hours and minutes.

Scoring Information
Give a total score of 0, 1, or 2.
Give a score of 1 for the correct answer.
Give a score of 0 or 1 for the working.

Q53.
Answer
20,000 ml

Work
The work should show an understanding that there are 1,000 milliliters in a liter, and show the calculation of $20 \times 1,000 = 20,000$.

Scoring Information
Give a total score of 0, 1, or 2.
Give a score of 1 for the correct answer.
Give a score of 0 or 1 for the working.

Q54.
Answer
110° or 110 degrees

Scoring Information
Give a total score of 0, 1, or 2.
Give a score of 1 for the correct numerical answer of 110.
Give a score of 1 for including the degrees symbol or the word degrees.

Q55.
Part A
Answer
5,147

Work
The work should show the calculation of 2,629 + 2,518 = 5,147.

Part B
Answer
111

Work
The work should show the calculation of 2,629 − 2,518 = 111.

Scoring Information
Give a total score of 0, 1, or 2.
Give a score of 1 for the correct answer to Part A.
Give a score of 1 for the correct answer to Part B.

Q56.
Answer
55°

Work
The work should show an understanding that there are 180° in a triangle and subtract 90° and 35° from 180° to give the missing angle measure of 55°.

Scoring Information
Give a total score of 0, 1, or 2.
Give a score of 1 for the correct answer.
Give a score of 0 or 1 for the working.

Q57.
Part A
Answer
The student should plot a point at 1.75, as shown below.

Part B
Answer
$1\frac{3}{4}$ or $1\frac{75}{100}$

Explanation
The student may describe using the number line to determine the fraction, or may describe a numerical conversion of the decimal to a fraction.

Scoring Information
Give a total score of 0, 1, 2, or 3.
Give a score of 1 for the correct answer to Part A.
Give a score of 1 for the correct answer to Part B.
Give a score of 0 or 1 for the explanation.

Q58.
Part A
Answer
The model should be shaded as shown below.

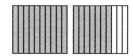

Part B
Answer
$\dfrac{17}{10}$

Explanation
The student may describe using the model to determine the improper fraction, or may describe a numerical conversion.

Scoring Information
Give a total score of 0, 1, 2, or 3.
Give a score of 1 for the correct answer to Part A.
Give a score of 1 for the correct answer to Part B.
Give a score of 0 or 1 for the explanation.

Q59.
Part A
Answer
41

Part B
The student should explain that each number in the pattern is 6 more than the one before it, and that the next number is found by adding 6 to the last number, 35.

Scoring Information
Give a total score of 0, 1, 2, or 3.
Give a score of 1 for the correct answer.
Give a score of 0, 1, or 2 for the explanation.

Q60.
Part A
Answer
The isosceles triangle in the center should be circled.

Part B
Explanation
The student may describe how the two halves are the same size and shape or how the two halves can be folded onto each other.

Scoring Information
Give a total score of 0, 1, 2, or 3.
Give a score of 1 for the correct shape circled.
Give a score of 0, 1, or 2 for the explanation.

Common Core Mathematics, Practice Test 2, Book 1

Question	Answer	Topic	Common Core Skill
1	B	Measurement & Data	Use the four operations to solve word problems involving time.
2	B	Operations/Algebraic Thinking	Solve multistep word problems posed with whole numbers and having whole-number answers using the four operations, including problems in which remainders must be interpreted.
3	D	Operations/Algebraic Thinking	Find all factor pairs for a whole number in the range 1–100. / Determine whether a given whole number in the range 1–100 is prime or composite.
4	A	Operations/Algebraic Thinking	Represent problems using equations with a letter standing for the unknown quantity.
5	C	Number & Operations-Fractions	Understand addition and subtraction of fractions as joining and separating parts referring to the same whole.
6	B	Operations/Algebraic Thinking	Find all factor pairs for a whole number in the range 1–100.
7	B	Operations/Algebraic Thinking	Assess the reasonableness of answers using mental computation and estimation strategies including rounding.
8	A	Operations/Algebraic Thinking	Solve multistep word problems posed with whole numbers and having whole-number answers using the four operations.
9	C	Measurement & Data	Use the four operations to solve word problems involving money.
10	C	Measurement & Data	Know relative sizes of measurement units within one system of units.
11	D	Operations/Algebraic Thinking	Find all factor pairs for a whole number in the range 1–100. / Determine whether a given whole number in the range 1–100 is prime or composite.
12	C	Operations/Algebraic Thinking	Generate and analyze patterns.
13	C	Measurement & Data	Solve problems by using information presented in line plots.
14	D	Number & Operations-Fractions	Understand, recognize, and generate equivalent fractions using visual fraction models, with attention to how the number and size of the parts differ even though the two fractions themselves are the same size.
15	D	Number & Operations in Base Ten	Recognize that in a multi-digit whole number, a digit in one place represents ten times what it represents in the place to its right.
16	C	Number & Operations-Fractions	Use decimal notation for fractions with denominators 10 or 100.
17	A	Number & Operations-Fractions	Record the results of comparisons with symbols >, =, or <, and justify the conclusions, e.g., by using a visual fraction model.
18	C	Operations/Algebraic Thinking	Assess the reasonableness of answers using mental computation and estimation strategies including rounding.

19	B	Measurement & Data	Within a single system of measurement, express measurements in a larger unit in terms of a smaller unit.
20	B	Measurement & Data	Measure angles in whole-number degrees using a protractor.
21	A	Operations/Algebraic Thinking	Generate and analyze patterns.
22	A	Number & Operations-Fractions	Use decimal notation for fractions with denominators 10 or 100.
23	C	Geometry	Identify perpendicular and parallel lines in two-dimensional figures.
24	A	Geometry	Identify line-symmetric figures and draw lines of symmetry.
25	D	Operations/Algebraic Thinking	Represent verbal statements of multiplicative comparisons as multiplication equations.

Common Core Mathematics, Practice Test 2, Book 2

Question	Answer	Topic	Common Core Skill
26	A	Geometry	Recognize right triangles as a category, and identify right triangles.
27	B	Number & Operations-Fractions	Decompose a fraction into a sum of fractions with the same denominator in more than one way, recording each decomposition by an equation.
28	D	Number & Operations in Base Ten	Compare two multi-digit numbers based on meanings of the digits in each place.
29	A	Number & Operations in Base Ten	Find whole-number quotients using strategies based on place value, the properties of operations, and/or the relationship between multiplication and division.
30	D	Measurement & Data	Know relative sizes of measurement units within one system of units.
31	D	Number & Operations-Fractions	Understand, recognize, and generate equivalent fractions using visual fraction models, with attention to how the number and size of the parts differ even though the two fractions themselves are the same size.
32	C	Operations/Algebraic Thinking	Generate and analyze patterns.
33	D	Number & Operations in Base Ten	Read and write multi-digit whole numbers using base-ten numerals, number names, and expanded form.
34	C	Measurement & Data	Represent measurement quantities using diagrams such as number line diagrams that feature a measurement scale.
35	C	Number & Operations in Base Ten	Recognize that in a multi-digit whole number, a digit in one place represents ten times what it represents in the place to its right.
36	B	Number & Operations-Fractions	Use decimal notation for fractions with denominators 10 or 100.
37	D	Measurement & Data	Use the four operations to solve word problems involving time.
38	C	Number & Operations-Fractions	Compare two decimals to hundredths by reasoning about their size.
39	D	Operations/Algebraic Thinking	Generate and analyze patterns.
40	B	Measurement & Data	Know relative sizes of measurement units within one system of units.
41	B	Measurement & Data	Use the four operations to solve word problems involving distances, including problems involving simple fractions or decimals.
42	B	Number & Operations-Fractions	Solve word problems involving multiplication of a fraction by a whole number.
43	C	Operations/Algebraic Thinking	Generate and analyze patterns.
44	A	Number & Operations in Base Ten	Find whole-number quotients using strategies based on place value, the properties of operations, and/or the relationship between multiplication and division.
45	A	Number & Operations in Base Ten	Read and write multi-digit whole numbers using base-ten numerals, number names, and expanded form.

46	B	Measurement & Data	Recognize angles as geometric shapes that are formed wherever two rays share a common endpoint.
47	B	Measurement & Data	Solve problems by using information presented in line plots.
48	A	Number & Operations in Base Ten	Recognize that in a multi-digit whole number, a digit in one place represents ten times what it represents in the place to its right.
49	A	Number & Operations-Fractions	Compare two decimals to hundredths by reasoning about their size.
50	B	Number & Operations-Fractions	Use decimal notation for fractions with denominators 10 or 100.

Common Core Mathematics, Practice Test 2, Book 3

Question	Points	Topic	Common Core Skill
51	2	Operations/Algebraic Thinking	Find all factor pairs for a whole number in the range 1–100.
52	2	Operations/Algebraic Thinking	Solve multistep word problems posed with whole numbers and having whole-number answers using the four operations, including problems in which remainders must be interpreted.
53	2	Number & Operations in Base Ten	Fluently add and subtract multi-digit whole numbers using the standard algorithm.
54	2	Number & Operations-Fractions	Compare two decimals to hundredths by reasoning about their size.
55	2	Measurement & Data	Apply the area and perimeter formulas for rectangles in real world and mathematical problems.
56	2	Measurement & Data	Use the four operations to solve word problems involving money.
57	3	Operations/Algebraic Thinking	Multiply or divide to solve word problems involving multiplicative comparison.
58	3	Measurement & Data	Sketch angles of specified measure.
59	3	Operations/Algebraic Thinking	Determine whether a given whole number in the range 1–100 is prime or composite.
60	3	Measurement & Data	Apply the area and perimeter formulas for rectangles in real world and mathematical problems.

Q51.
Answer
1, 2, 5, 10

Work
The work may list the factors of each number, may show factor trees, or may show an understanding that 10 is a factor of 20 and 40, and so all the factors of 10 are common factors of 10, 20, and 40.

Scoring Information
Give a total score of 0, 1, or 2.
Give a score of 1 for the correct answer.
Give a score of 0 or 1 for the working.

Q52.
Answer
10 pencils

Work
The work should show the calculation of $82 \div 8 = 10$ remainder 2.

Scoring Information
Give a total score of 0, 1, or 2.
Give a score of 1 for the correct answer.
Give a score of 0 or 1 for the working.

Q53.
Answer
718

Work
The work should show the calculation of 254 + 235 + 229 = 718.

Scoring Information
Give a total score of 0, 1, or 2.
Give a score of 1 for the correct answer.
Give a score of 0 or 1 for the working.

Q54.
Answer
July, May, April, June

Scoring Information
Give a total score of 0, 1, or 2.
Give a score of 2 for a completely correct answer.
Give a score of 1 if 2 or 3 months are ordered correctly.
Give a score of 0 if 0 or 1 months are ordered correctly.

Q55.
Answer
4 square inches or 4 in^2

Work
The work should show the side length as 2 inches, and show the calculation of 2 inches × 2 inches = 4 square inches.

Scoring Information
Give a total score of 0, 1, or 2.
Give a score of 1 for the correct numerical answer of 4.
Give a score of 1 for the correct units of square inches or in^2.

Q56.
Answer
15 nickels

Work
The work may show that each quarter is equal to 25 cents, or 5 nickels, and then show 5 × 3 = 15. The work may also show that the quarters are equal to 75 cents, and a nickel is equal to 5 cents, and then show the calculation 75 ÷ 5 = 15.

Scoring Information
Give a total score of 0, 1, or 2.
Give a score of 1 for the correct answer.
Give a score of 0 or 1 for the working.

Q57.
Part A
Answer
6

Work
The work should show that 6 is the greatest number that divides evenly into 12, 18, and 24.

Part B
Answer
4

Work
The work may show the calculation of 24 ÷ 6 = 4, or could use a diagram to represent 6 piles of 4 pennies each.

Scoring Information
Give a total score of 0, 1, 2, or 3.
Give a score of 1 for the correct answer to Part A.
Give a score of 1 for the correct answer to Part B.
Give a score of 0 or 1 for the working.

Q58.
The student should sketch a labeled right angle with an angle equal to 90°.
The student should sketch a labeled acute angle with an angle less than 90°.
The student should sketch a labeled obtuse angle with an angle greater than 90°.

Scoring Information
Give a total score of 0, 1, 2, or 3.
Give a score of 1 for each angle correctly sketched.

Q59.
The student should list the numbers 23 and 29.

Explanation
The student should explain that prime numbers can only be divided by themselves and 1, while composite numbers can be divided by at least one other number.

Scoring Information
Give a total score of 0, 1, 2, or 3.
Give a score of 1 for each number correctly listed. Take off 1 point for each additional number incorrectly listed.
Give a score of 0 or 1 for the explanation.

Q60.
Part A
Answer
240 feet

Work
The work should show the calculation of 80 + 80 + 40 + 40 = 240 or (2 × 80) + (2 × 40) = 240.

Part B
Answer
80 yards

Work
The work should show an understanding that there are 3 feet in 1 yard.
The work should show the calculation of 240 ÷ 3 = 80.

Scoring Information
Give a total score of 0, 1, 2, or 3.
Give a score of 1 for the correct answer to Part A.
Give a score of 1 for the correct answer to Part B.
Give a score of 0 or 1 for the working.

Answer Sheet: Practice Test 1

Book 1				Book 2			
1	Ⓐ Ⓑ Ⓒ Ⓓ	16	Ⓐ Ⓑ Ⓒ Ⓓ	26	Ⓐ Ⓑ Ⓒ Ⓓ	41	Ⓐ Ⓑ Ⓒ Ⓓ
2	Ⓐ Ⓑ Ⓒ Ⓓ	17	Ⓐ Ⓑ Ⓒ Ⓓ	27	Ⓐ Ⓑ Ⓒ Ⓓ	42	Ⓐ Ⓑ Ⓒ Ⓓ
3	Ⓐ Ⓑ Ⓒ Ⓓ	18	Ⓐ Ⓑ Ⓒ Ⓓ	28	Ⓐ Ⓑ Ⓒ Ⓓ	43	Ⓐ Ⓑ Ⓒ Ⓓ
4	Ⓐ Ⓑ Ⓒ Ⓓ	19	Ⓐ Ⓑ Ⓒ Ⓓ	29	Ⓐ Ⓑ Ⓒ Ⓓ	44	Ⓐ Ⓑ Ⓒ Ⓓ
5	Ⓐ Ⓑ Ⓒ Ⓓ	20	Ⓐ Ⓑ Ⓒ Ⓓ	30	Ⓐ Ⓑ Ⓒ Ⓓ	45	Ⓐ Ⓑ Ⓒ Ⓓ
6	Ⓐ Ⓑ Ⓒ Ⓓ	21	Ⓐ Ⓑ Ⓒ Ⓓ	31	Ⓐ Ⓑ Ⓒ Ⓓ	46	Ⓐ Ⓑ Ⓒ Ⓓ
7	Ⓐ Ⓑ Ⓒ Ⓓ	22	Ⓐ Ⓑ Ⓒ Ⓓ	32	Ⓐ Ⓑ Ⓒ Ⓓ	47	Ⓐ Ⓑ Ⓒ Ⓓ
8	Ⓐ Ⓑ Ⓒ Ⓓ	23	Ⓐ Ⓑ Ⓒ Ⓓ	33	Ⓐ Ⓑ Ⓒ Ⓓ	48	Ⓐ Ⓑ Ⓒ Ⓓ
9	Ⓐ Ⓑ Ⓒ Ⓓ	24	Ⓐ Ⓑ Ⓒ Ⓓ	34	Ⓐ Ⓑ Ⓒ Ⓓ	49	Ⓐ Ⓑ Ⓒ Ⓓ
10	Ⓐ Ⓑ Ⓒ Ⓓ	25	Ⓐ Ⓑ Ⓒ Ⓓ	35	Ⓐ Ⓑ Ⓒ Ⓓ	50	Ⓐ Ⓑ Ⓒ Ⓓ
11	Ⓐ Ⓑ Ⓒ Ⓓ			36	Ⓐ Ⓑ Ⓒ Ⓓ		
12	Ⓐ Ⓑ Ⓒ Ⓓ			37	Ⓐ Ⓑ Ⓒ Ⓓ		
13	Ⓐ Ⓑ Ⓒ Ⓓ			38	Ⓐ Ⓑ Ⓒ Ⓓ		
14	Ⓐ Ⓑ Ⓒ Ⓓ			39	Ⓐ Ⓑ Ⓒ Ⓓ		
15	Ⓐ Ⓑ Ⓒ Ⓓ			40	Ⓐ Ⓑ Ⓒ Ⓓ		

Book 3

Write the answers to the questions in Book 3 in your test book.

Answer Sheet: Practice Test 2

Book 1				Book 2			
1	Ⓐ Ⓑ Ⓒ Ⓓ	**16**	Ⓐ Ⓑ Ⓒ Ⓓ	**26**	Ⓐ Ⓑ Ⓒ Ⓓ	**41**	Ⓐ Ⓑ Ⓒ Ⓓ
2	Ⓐ Ⓑ Ⓒ Ⓓ	**17**	Ⓐ Ⓑ Ⓒ Ⓓ	**27**	Ⓐ Ⓑ Ⓒ Ⓓ	**42**	Ⓐ Ⓑ Ⓒ Ⓓ
3	Ⓐ Ⓑ Ⓒ Ⓓ	**18**	Ⓐ Ⓑ Ⓒ Ⓓ	**28**	Ⓐ Ⓑ Ⓒ Ⓓ	**43**	Ⓐ Ⓑ Ⓒ Ⓓ
4	Ⓐ Ⓑ Ⓒ Ⓓ	**19**	Ⓐ Ⓑ Ⓒ Ⓓ	**29**	Ⓐ Ⓑ Ⓒ Ⓓ	**44**	Ⓐ Ⓑ Ⓒ Ⓓ
5	Ⓐ Ⓑ Ⓒ Ⓓ	**20**	Ⓐ Ⓑ Ⓒ Ⓓ	**30**	Ⓐ Ⓑ Ⓒ Ⓓ	**45**	Ⓐ Ⓑ Ⓒ Ⓓ
6	Ⓐ Ⓑ Ⓒ Ⓓ	**21**	Ⓐ Ⓑ Ⓒ Ⓓ	**31**	Ⓐ Ⓑ Ⓒ Ⓓ	**46**	Ⓐ Ⓑ Ⓒ Ⓓ
7	Ⓐ Ⓑ Ⓒ Ⓓ	**22**	Ⓐ Ⓑ Ⓒ Ⓓ	**32**	Ⓐ Ⓑ Ⓒ Ⓓ	**47**	Ⓐ Ⓑ Ⓒ Ⓓ
8	Ⓐ Ⓑ Ⓒ Ⓓ	**23**	Ⓐ Ⓑ Ⓒ Ⓓ	**33**	Ⓐ Ⓑ Ⓒ Ⓓ	**48**	Ⓐ Ⓑ Ⓒ Ⓓ
9	Ⓐ Ⓑ Ⓒ Ⓓ	**24**	Ⓐ Ⓑ Ⓒ Ⓓ	**34**	Ⓐ Ⓑ Ⓒ Ⓓ	**49**	Ⓐ Ⓑ Ⓒ Ⓓ
10	Ⓐ Ⓑ Ⓒ Ⓓ	**25**	Ⓐ Ⓑ Ⓒ Ⓓ	**35**	Ⓐ Ⓑ Ⓒ Ⓓ	**50**	Ⓐ Ⓑ Ⓒ Ⓓ
11	Ⓐ Ⓑ Ⓒ Ⓓ			**36**	Ⓐ Ⓑ Ⓒ Ⓓ		
12	Ⓐ Ⓑ Ⓒ Ⓓ			**37**	Ⓐ Ⓑ Ⓒ Ⓓ		
13	Ⓐ Ⓑ Ⓒ Ⓓ			**38**	Ⓐ Ⓑ Ⓒ Ⓓ		
14	Ⓐ Ⓑ Ⓒ Ⓓ			**39**	Ⓐ Ⓑ Ⓒ Ⓓ		
15	Ⓐ Ⓑ Ⓒ Ⓓ			**40**	Ⓐ Ⓑ Ⓒ Ⓓ		

Book 3

Write the answers to the questions in Book 3 in your test book.

Made in the USA
San Bernardino, CA
27 October 2016